The Root Endures

The Root Endures

Poems

Jeff Burt

Sheila-Na-Gig Editions

ISBN: 978-1-962405-58-4
Library of Congress Control Number: 2026930288

Sheila-Na-Gig Editions
Russell, KY
Hayley Mitchell Haugen, Editor
www.sheilanagigblog.com

Acknowledgments

Afterthepause: "Into the Standing Grain"
Amethyst Review: "Prayer Shawl"
Barnwood: "Passage"
Boomer Lit Mag: "Waxworks"
Clerestory Poetry Journal: "By Moving I Remain"
Cold Mountain Review: "We Will Never Mend This"
Crab Creek Journal: "Using Rust as Pigment"
Dandelion Farm Review: "June Swoon"
Divot: A Journal of Poetry: "At the Window in Spring"
Eclectica Magazine: "One-way, Out and Only"
Farmer-ish: "Near Lime Bog," "Snow Fence"
Friends of Poetry: "Minor Morning"
Heartwood Literary Magazine: "Barn, Moth," "The Infinitive to
    Listen," "To My Child"
Kestrel: A Journal of Literature and Art: "My Grandfather
    Recalls Letters from My Mother"
Mineral Lit Mag: "Question for Van Gogh"
Mused Bella: "Holsteins at Equinox"
Paddler Press: "Keel and Song"
Phren-z: "Walking Zayante Sandhills"
Rabid Oak: "Stilt-walker," "The Large Swales in the Road"
Red Wolf Journal: "Trestle"
Sheila-Na-Gig online: "Mudroom," "Purity," "Signature,"
    "Two Nights Past the Summer Solstice," "Written on
    Walt Whitman's Birthday"
Sixfold: "Metronome," "Tribute to Phyllis"
Sunlight Press: "The Other Shoe"
Terrene Magazine: "Midas"
ucity review: "The Root Endures, a Poem from Home"
Vita Poetica: "Jonah"
Watershed Review: "In Honor of Big-Bellied Men," "There is
    Nothing Except"
Williwaw Journal: "Four Novembers," "Lime Bog," "Rusk
    County Rag"

Willows Wept Review: "As if Copper Wire Sang the Unleashing of Time," "Everything Rural Will Be Razed," "Richland Centre, Wisconsin," "Vigil"
Word Soup: "The Calling"
Written Tales Magazine: "One Rung Down"
Zingara Poetry Review: "Removing a Gate"

Dedication

I would like to dedicate this work to and thank Cori and my children, who have brought a staggering and sustaining beauty to my life, and to my parents and my wife's parents, who have been the stems from which I have continued to grow.

Contents

The Unleashing of Time

The Calling

By Moving I Remain

The Root Endures

The Unleashing of Time

Minor Morning

I am one who waits in the minor morning
which has the silence
of a stone, a minor morning
with the heaviness of a stone, a minor morning
with the silent song of stone
in the less-than-wished-for minor morning.
In this less than light we know as morning
the first of solar fire
seems delayed, the immensest kiss of fire
which will break the minor morning
seems delayed, the strings
of yellow light not yet strings

which could sound, strings
silent in the minor morning—
like guitar strings
unstrung, or mandolin strings
in silence,
mandolin propped on a shelf, or strings
like the strings
of a lyre, the player asleep on stone,
strings as heavy as stone,
strings
of the kiss of the immensest fire.
I am one who waits for this fire

to erase a fire
from a star expelling light in strings
of fire,
star perched in air like a pin on a map, a minor fire
in the minor morning.
As I wait a fire
from night's rage dies in my heart, a fire
which falls to silence
and the silence

is full, and the fire
fades to have the sound of a stone,
but not the heaviness of a stone,
for a stone
has the silence
of a song not sung and a stone
has the heaviness of that song, a stone
like a song stuck in the chest, unsung. Strings
of the throat which could sing out the stone
of song and the heaviness of the stone
in the minor morning
before the morning
we know as morning (without the heaviness of stone)
these strings do not sing, for they are in silence
as a stone is in silence.

I am one who waits in this silence
still as a stone.
I watch in silence
and this heavy, heavy silence
is like a kiss without fire.
The silence
unready for song builds to a greater silence.
Then the strings
of that great lyre of morning approach, strings
of the morning
we know as morning,
not the minor morning.

Morning
silence
gives way to wind over stone.
Fire!
I play my strings.

Rusk County Rag

A fourth-grader, I had run away, or maybe just run,
and now had to come running back
to the nettles of my grandmother's speech,
grandfather exhausted and sad from searching block after block,
but I had news to tell, a trampled field, a far-flung farm
and now comprehending loss, that I was lost,
clothes rumpled, rambling and rumbling
through the rural decay of Rusk County, rust and ruin,
like a big-bellied-boar rooting up a backyard,
enraptured by pitchfork-piled haystacks, corncribs and pig-shacks,
and in a half-dug hole a skull and rump bone of cow,

I had stumbled sputtering vulgar words too robust
for a thin boy, all knuckles and buckles,
and the shallow fields of new winter wheat and grazed corn,
cattail ditches and duckweed ponds
made my voice a thunderous drum,
I had come full of bunk and beauty knowing plugs
to lure bass-thumps at dusk,
stump-sitting, fence-jumping, tunnels and fox-run,
wigwam, wigwag, zigzag and scram,
delving in depths for crayfish, crawdad, tadpole and toad.

And as I traipsed, I took in the sky blue and precise
behind each definite thing as if I could pocket it,
then broke down with a shudder, a shake,
swallowed by the immensity of each definite thing,
and as I walked toward my grandfather's home
all pants and chance, I walked on the path
by the Flambeau, river of flowing flames.
In the water the autumn hues mingled,
refracted, reflected, drawn deeper by water.
The land flowed slowly where I stood.
The river stood still.
The tamarack and cedar, maple and aspen,

white birch and black birch, paper birch unbound,
boxwood and oak, butternut, elm,
all danced in rapture without wind.

Feverish and hollow, struck dumb
by the ringing bell of the Flambeau,
I knew this wending ribbon
of water had deceived, had deked
and tricked and taken my spirit with fire.

I remember the river flickering like embers at evening,
the swallows and martins following the lines
of the shore with cries of sharp trepidation,
martins in threes, swallows in throngs,
my immense jubilation, as if pleasure persisted
by the intimate beating of wings.

Purity

I wasn't good at listening, my mother said,
though I could hear just fine,
because listening meant obeying,
and other times it meant understanding in the moment
and then obeying tomorrow or whenever
that moment came again, or listening meant
a revelation could occur if I was quiet
and sitting still, like waiting for the crush
of a hoof on a leaf and then seeing a deer
poke its nose out of the arbor.

Truth was like that sometimes, she said,
not like a math equation where it solves
all kinds of problems, or a science discovery
that cures or changes how we are with things,
not the pulpits' shall and shall nots,
but like Dr. King when his voice pierced the rain
from underneath his umbrella
and a glimpse of sunshine came from his words,
or listening to the way Rudy Schwartz sang
head bent over left with a wide-open mouth
and his shoes bent from tippy-toes.
When you listen, you'll think of purity, she said,
of the clear cold water of the artesian spring
by the creek by the mill
just after it crosses under the highway
on the south side of the hill on a warm day.

June Swoon

Just beyond the dangling lashes of catalpa,
     in the dim reaches of the leafy interior
where you and larvae lounge in the litter
     of spring, pupae and pupil, a human sparrow
in the secluded thicket, you recount
     how it started, straying from the path
to the last day of school, drawn by the light
     of button weed and butterwort, bluebells
and Johnny jump-ups, that led to the foal
     so full of kick, camber, gallop and camp
you believed her mother was a mare
     and her father the wind, huge, warm,
invitingly wild, hooves as hard as feathers,
     you recount how the foal led to a fence
and the light of the high sky where baseballs
     disappear, the heat fused to the field
and wavering off asphalt, you try to recount
     how it happened, but you know you will never
get it right, you will never explain
     how you were held for hours watching
dust devils on the infield and thunder
     at the plate, in love with the twinkle of sweat
dripping off a black man's brow.

As If Copper Wire Sang the Unleashing of Time

I woke in the dark the birds light with song
hoping to sleep sloped against the door
        or cold window of the car

on the road to the lake but never did sleep,
the pale steeples and silent belfries rising
        in the stars and Gromme's pond

a murky mirror, the maple, alder and oak
so still they moved mysteriously out of focus
        like the gaze of a storyteller.

Dad slipped the boat in the lake and dropped the motor silently,
no fuller grace than this he had. Black and blue the water shone,
        stretched and broken back

over rounded rocks and creosote-soaked pillars,
lilies white opening clouds in the flat green pads
        rolling with the seiche

of the lake, rush and reed, pondweed, and pickerelweed
wavering in the wake of the wave and the wash brimming
        with bright chlorophyll.

The smell of metal followed us everywhere-
oarlocks, bait box, bailing tins, dare
        devils, zebras, abus

and black lunch pails, treble hooks, gaff hooks,
chain net, clasp and zipper. Before the sun swam
        over the trees the sky

resembled the blue sheen of the blackbird's wing,
the sky gathered and swarmed and entered my chest
        and I wished for the grace of a hawk

to show what had been given, but my spirit stuttered.
Deepened once, I looked to the lake and dark smooth
           life rolled through me,

the lake swept, the roiling of waters
and the pillars of mist tinged with points of light
           at the swell and the trough

black and in-between varying shades of gray
and purple and blue and I knew the burning voice
           of God the wonder in my own time.

At the water's edge, land and lake were not separable,
an eerie seamless zone where a growth of trees
           did not mean I had reached the shore.

Near the cove we would beach the boat
and hike to a slough where minnows and rotifers
           abounded, but no fish.

We'd reel through brush, drunk to their touch.
Tensed to the prick, we'd wince with a joy
           when blackberry bramble

scraped at our pants, nettles pierced our palms.
We were lost to the lake, and became like the fish—
           so roused the lily, chased

the frog, the blue dragonflies, and flipped our feathery-bait
like an arcing ball for a snap at a hand-tied fly.
           Sunrise, Dad would say,

as if time were audible. I would be ripping
up a rock, shredding the moss off, grabbing albino grubs,
           then lying face down

nose snug to the grass hearing dark fish
near cozening pads slapping the lake like cowpokes
      clapping their hands in a rowdy bar,

and the wing-scraped chords of lacewings elegantly rising
like violins approaching crescendo, and knew Dad heard
      this as clear as if copper wire sang

the unleashing of time, time now and time eternal
made audible in the hum and buzz of things risen
      and fallen in the twilight.

He could make me take a breath deep and slow
and hold it, and as sunlight flared in all the fanning leaves
      and dewdrops became plumes of praise and vines

as frangible pipettes brilliant with a chemistry
of such intricate elements as quiet light and burnished water
      and delicate air,

the difficult trick was to remember the bobber,
the nibbles on the line and the twist of the hook
      which told turtle bite

or vulnerable gill, and Dad could do
a more difficult trick by bobbing between
      the unfurling fanfare

of a world given to light and the twinge and yank
of fishing with a purpose. When he went under
      he was under, whether

in reverie or reality while I rode red a little
white a little, tugged and sampled, looking at his face
      for markers, buoys, a way.

Right shoulder slumped and rounded by dislocation,
Appalachian mound to his rocky left peak,
          he once told me

"If I didn't have your mother and you kids I'd never leave
these waters." I felt the words not numbed by terror
          of truth revealed,

for his arms were love and they held me high
to the branch holding my hook, the leaves with my line,
          for his legs were the trunk

and I was part of his reaching, the whispered words
were the lights that dance at the conclusion of leaves.
          He must have come to the lake needing nothing more

than to be part of the lake and having been part, to part.
When we'd come home pan fish in pail for pictures and gutting,
          his furrows would re-form

and break his enraptured face and I used to think if only
the heart were broken, so you could throw away the aching half,
          but a heart only cracks.

It was here at the lake the tongue went crazy with words,
all the hushed and whispered rhymes and analogues,
          dialogues with rod and self.

Language may die like a river entering the chaos of the sea,
but like a lake it is born of springs of artesian images,
          the tongue in love with the shape of vowels

fricatives, phonemes and syllables and sense,
in love with the merest drop of liquid speech oozing through
          a darn's crack. It was here in the cold rosy comfort

of the mid-morning sun and the lake gone still
and the wind gone with it that words came up
            to conserve and clarify the world, the words

a repository of all the tributaries entering a life,
a solvent for settling the solid and buoying the airy,
            scrubbing the soiled, babbling tongue breaking

over the lock of meter, roaring voice cracking the dam of time.
Visions were rhythms, images took root as sound,
            myth and legend made by the accent

from the springs of wonder converging with the soul
of speech, minor acts become immense at the primitive frontier
            of history and dream, in modulation

and mooring of syntax and syllable. And the lake, passive,
like the sentences children write still struck by things
            and nouns because their bodies and minds

are always motive, before they learn the newsy grammar
of active voice, the lake slipping over pebbles and rocks
            propelled by the winds, settling over rocks

worn smooth as if learning a language,
the ways of grammar, not sentences or specific and concrete
            words, but rules of order, of rocks and dissolution,

as if the lake which destroys, as if the lake seeks
to learn the process of creation it wears down,
            and by learning, seeks to restore, to build.

Dawn, dawn and the world of houses
left for the hull of a boat, pillow and dream
            for mist and whispers

of eternity, dawn and a three-foot pickerel
thrashing in the net, its pattern of links
        suggesting a chain of events

become one, a crack of depth in the shallows,
substance below the surface of thought, a bobber pulled under,
        time yanked out of time.

We used to cast our line one last time
 to unkink the snarls, we used to cast
        one last time several times

just to linger at the lake, the way lovers
fused to the field of ardor kiss once,
        then, again and again.

Tribute to Phyllis

She punished the laundry, scraping the jeans of her boys
knuckles white against the washboard
flapped and snapped dishtowels and rags like a randy bully
in the high school shower against the butt of the basin
and clipped the clothespins with revenge to hold the sheets
that had been bleached and softened and breeze dried.

She could make shirts weep and undershirts cry
and boxers mourn as they pinned on the line.
Disease flew from her ferocity, and comfort came
when she'd hold the swaddling clothes to her nose
and sniff and smile as if something holy had taken place.
When she walked down the river the rocks remembered
and the riprap still murmurs her praise.

Ode on a Yard Light

By five in the afternoon in December
the yard light, hung from a pole, turned on
over where the tractor stood
at the entrance to the barn,
a corn-picker idle since September,
a plow waiting for snow, and a backhoe,
a yard not as in sown grass
but as in railroad or barn
where all the engines are kept,
checked in and out.

I had been left at a farm by my parents
for Christmas break
as a way to teach me hard work,
and though the work was hard,
the lesson I learned was being left.
All night I would toss and turn
and see the yard light pouring
through the curtains like moonlight
in spring keeps one awake,
then rise at dawn for chores and see it
still casting radiance all around.

It was a dark time,
and I treasured the light
cast all around me.

Into the Standing Grain

Stunned by sunrise,
shocked by a school bus
with torn brown seats
and dirt clods on the floor,
I rode with twenty other sleepy teenagers
to a corn field to detassel one cob
to encourage the sex of another,
juveniles delinquent,
punished by work.

Swarms of sweetness
flowed over the field,
dew sliding magnifiers
on the curling leaves
that razor-sliced
forearms uncovered.
By mid-morning,
moisture lifted, chaff
flew and stuck,
cuff-wedged,
crease-hid,
jammed into socks
and eyelets on tennis shoes
and boots, as if we
were walking rods of epoxy.
We withstood smut,
rust and worm
to eat peanut butter,
bologna, spam,
stale chips
washed by Kool-Aid
or synthetic lemonade.
Jugs came in one size,
large, one color,
a baked-out blue.

Our foreman identified
the silk as beard,
by August burned black
at the end of the ear,
but to fingers the silk
was a girl's hair,
a satin dress,
legs you were denied,
but any joke of sex
he quickly broke
with "back to work,"
a quick jump up.
He had done time,
my mother told me,
for defending his daughter,
beat a bull
who had deflowered her,
left a schoolteacher,
returned a con,
found work only
weeding out the rogues
and driving the discarded bus.
Townspeople avoided
conversation with him
the way two like poles
of a magnet repel.

Work ended at two
when the bus stopped
at the old brick creamery
held up by mortar
and the fatigue the town had
in tearing it down,
handles of churns
mounted in the windows.
I walked home
with the foreman and often

the only sound between us
was the plastic clatter
of our jugs against each other,
he with a little hitch
to the right and I
a little hitch to the left,
lunch pails
slapping our thighs,
lightened, empty,
happy as puppies
wagging by our sides.

As we'd pass the final corner
on Cathcart, we would eye
the horizon for tomorrow's weather,
I prayed for rain,
for a muddy field.
He looked for clear skies,
for work, past the last hills
for a small town's humility,
for healing, for grace.

In Honor of Big-Bellied Men

The shotgun flap of the large gray noodle of belt
running the generator punctuated the loud hum
of the engine itself, and the conveyor spun

its elongated oval dumping grist at one end,
conveying shucked pig corn on the other,
the chaff and the pixie dust dancing above it

in the spotlights the missing knots in the walls allowed.
Greetings were yelled by men with bibs
and muscular bellies broad and protruding,

the right gut for pushing a fence into place
or containing a cow bent on leaving the barn
spooked by a rat covered by feed,

bellies that could take the sweaty head of a boy
or girl at twilight when the bats swooped in
and give them comfort, secure the world,

bellies that could hold a baby without a lap,
that pushed hay and milk and bushels of beets
out into a dangerous and starving world.

Stilt-walker

The roofers called me gopher, grunt,
the job requiring the obedience of a loyal retriever
and the resilience from continual deprecation,
the skinny kid hired for a few weeks
of summer when the temperatures arced
and the sun rose hot and discomfort with it.

I'd carry two bundles of shingles
up a ladder past the second story dormers
and drop them to the roof with a bark
that was half detonation of a shell
and half the first syllable of a growl
of an angry dog. I would tip forward

slightly to unload and the lightening
would tilt the ladder away from the house,
and in momentary rapture I'd stand
like the world's tallest man on stilts
before the lean of my arms would bring
the ladder back to the eaves waiting like a mother.

All rapture is like that, momentary,
a surprising balance of danger
and freedom from the weight of work.
Even today, I took a chance on the apex
of a ladder working to trim a privet,
needing to grab a higher branch to saw

the lower, and for a moment as the teeth
chunked soft wood from the branch
my toes left the metal rung
and I hung as I sawed, the thick branch broke
and fell with the same thud of a pack of shingles,
and I was happy, hanging above earth,

for again I had defeated gravity
with a fleeting circus act,
again, I was the walker on stilts.

The Calling

The Calling

If I can plunk the planks like piano keys,
make balance beams of iron tracks

until the earth has lost its daily dance;
if I can tramp the rail so far I'm alone

to things; if I can make the string of boxcars
on the spur like a home in the ubiquitous dark

by squatting in the dust and rust and dirt
of cold metal walls and wooden floors,

curling like fingers to a palm for warmth
and dream the locomotive of dawn, its bright

celestial clack in the cold black
medium of space, dream the dipper,

the drinking gourd, the California here
I come—when I wake and cannot see the sun

can I not rise and walk and risk the heart
to go out into confusion, and speak

to crows, gather wild lilies, spiderworts,
phlox, chicory, and ox-eye daisies,

everything which grows toward me,
shed the bondage and bandage of fear

for the rapture and rupture of joy,
burn as surrogate for the solar train,

the raucous roaring delicious imbecility
of creation, living an obligation to be light

Lime Bog

Entering Lime Bog for cranberries was difficult,
bramble like sidewinders looped and intersected
like rolls of barbed wire at a border.
Days in the fall during college when Dan and I'd visit
the cranberries would still be under water,
and then, pop, some would appear
on the surface on a Saturday morning,
we'd wade with heavy rubber gear,
swing our weighted legs out in half-circle
just to go forward with a step.
We did not need a rake or pole.
As our legs trudged cranberries would surface,
until we'd look back and see a twenty-foot-long
swath of red and orange. Boyish fun,
we were interested in making a line of red
against the backdrop of yellow foliage.
That was our harvest, simply the color.
But we burlap-bagged a few pounds,
took them to my landlord Mrs. Vovakovic
who made both a tart jam and relish.
Boys' joy in men's bodies.

In winter the third year of our discovery
I returned after snow had fallen
to look at the bog. The impenetrable bramble
now had openings that deer had made
that I could bend and follow
and only a few poking spears of vegetation
came through the snow and ice,
as if fingers motioning for assistance,
calling for help to churn the water,
for a pop and splash of red.

But Dan did not come, not hearty
for a long walk in the cold weather.

It's a bog, he yelled over the phone, a bog.
You visit a bog in autumn and no other time.
It needs time to sleep, and you're going to wake it.
Whether it was the cranberries aligned in a channel,
the vibrant red against the dying leaves
or the companionship of Dan I missed, I did not know.
Like a small child at the door to their parent's bedroom,
I went week after week, trying to rouse it.

Metronome

Nestled in the far distances
my imagination had roamed
in the nether land,
still, I am near to and nearing my home.
Frieda, my grandmotherly neighbor,
waves me in, the lost pilot
returning from the army air corps.
Yet after the fantasy recedes
its repercussions linger:
I step over a fence
and it rapidly disappears,
the steadily burgeoning sun
wades through formidable leaves,
air widens, and twilight shadows
fly over drought-shriveled grass.
The paint on a primitive church shines
pudgy and white,
billowing like a parachute.
I smile, listen:
the wood is not laughing.
In the dry hot wind button-black susans
tango and rock,
dust waltzes
to unheard-of music, Frieda's wave
a metronome of my heart.

With each thing both fanciful
and real, how flat the imagining man,
a solid body with spirit
which cannot by any artifice
detach itself from flesh
and vanish in a vaporous ascension
to the promise of joy.
How, when we can believe
all the feather, bone

and beak of our existence was born
of a central egg, can
we not set the mind skyward,
free in its flight?
Like gravity the daily routines
pull down magnificent creations,
and it is one continuum
between fancy and fact,
the two ends of the pole
with which we balance
unaware of any safety net,
the tipping of one end too high
sure to flip us off the wire.

So I feel: it is hot.
While there are no limits
to the distance a dream may take,
the clock of my body yanks
me back to the small seam
of time I continually try
to rip—a far journey
in a short span.
And though reentry
to the war-torn fortress
of a common world is loss,
an unshielded burning,
the greater intensity
of rapid associations
reduced to a linear conversation,
it is the condensation,
the subsequent recalling
of the imagined event
which makes the fantasy desired.
The ether I once was
vanishes, and I reappear
glistening and whole, joy
rising to the surface of my face,

death and logic submersing
to become a sediment
from which I can only toss and swell above.
I am liquid, a lake,
and the trickle from the hose
is a river replenishing
my arid head,
and a beer is the storm
dousing the kiln
of my thinning throat.

Waxworks

1/

My mother wanes under the burning penumbra
of the waxing October moon, walking away

the high tide of sweetness in her blood,
diabetes, like the name of a constellation

believed to silently influence a daily life,
diabetes, twin poles yanking her high and low,

always on the cusp of transformation
into platonic Jekyll or grinding Hyde.

I lose sight of her as the sound of the word
rises, a prayer for a syringe of magic,

a cure, though I know she has no rush of hope,
living with a fix, which, in truth, fixes nothing.

Today, amid the woods stripped of leaves,
we cut stems of the bittersweet,

plump dull-red arils under orange caps,
waxworks bobbing near barbed wire,

avoiding the woody nightshade
that is true bittersweet, its heart-shaped leaves

like the fist in the chest, no lovely valentine
cloistered over ill-formed fruit of poisonous scarlet,

the color of blood from her fingertip
when a quick blind stab draws it out.

2/

In the dew of the evening, I envision her walking,
the switch of her form turning darkened spears of grass

into light, as if all particles from celestial bodies
which have fallen to earth, absorbed by plant and sod,

had come back to life, radiant in their resurrection.
With everything once June-fat now fall-shorn

by the wind, I am braced by her beauty,
the elegance of her strain, the ornament of bare form,

the melodic evocation in her conversation,
and in my heart, both the fist in chest

and the place of mirth and remorse,
I feel the twisted waxworks unwinding,

fingers nested in the palm uncurling,
see how thin trees look without leaves

defined in the twilight by the merest of moon,
depleted, but no longer in need.

My Grandfather Recalls Letters from My Mother

She wrote of pencil marks on kitchen doorposts
marking your growth, woodpeckers on the maple,
squeak of swings, red wagon like a sunset.
She rhapsodized about being a bookkeeper
at a shoe store and an accounts keeper
at a small-town newspaper tracking insertions
and quarter-page ads and the deductions from barter
that Shrimp the publisher made daily,
bass fileted and buttered from the bait shop,
a pair of orange boots from the feed store
out on Highway 12, a Tuesday night dinner
of roast beef on toast from the town's only restaurant across the street.

She liked the discipline of a job, the waking
at a set hour as if she were a rooster needing
to crow the yard into morning, not walking
but striding at a fast pace to arrive five minutes early
to be at her desk exactly when the cranked clock struck eight.

She ate her lunch at little nooks where sparrows
and chickadees came and pecked at the cracker crumbs
and bread she'd spread on the pavement,
and at five would close her ledgers and cap her ink,
wear a kerchief if the wind had risen off the lake
where the paper mill churned pulp and matchsticks.
Every day except for the weather wonderfully the same.

Work was school, of course, she understood that,
the books, the ink, the promptness, the exactness
of the penny, the lonely lunchtimes and walk home,
and how she greeted her husband instead of father.
She could have lived all days as replicas
of the previous one and been happy.
Routine fulfilled her.
It was not the first pregnancy and birth that changed her,

being that one child could be folded
into the swaddling clothes of her regimen,
be scheduled, fed, bathed and nursed
according to the Franklin clock on the mantle.
It was the second pregnancy and birth,
the sickly child, the measles, chicken pox, scarlatina,
all before you were two, the rising early to care
while staying up late to care for the other,
and somewhere finding time in between
to write her father, to talk about flocks of blackbirds
and the sauce and canter of the grackles
clutching the conversation as if it were a precious jewel.

Chaos came. With two children, not only had time morphed
into hours that were longer than sixty minutes
and days that were shorter than twenty-four hours,
but seconds dragged, and weeks lost rhythm and meaning.
Bills came and the envelopes of cash didn't match,
the grocery money had to be borrowed from the heating stash
and the heating stash had to be borrowed
from the envelope for clothes and shoes
and the envelope for clothes and shoes
had to be fortified with money from vacation
and the envelope for vacation seemed perpetually open
for other envelopes to enjoy.

She would sit at her desk at the day's end
with a lamp casting its meager quivering
yellow incandescence upon her papers,
the inkwell gone to ballpoint, and cry,
cry without sound, and then she would write to me,
write to me how wonderful the day had been,
how a robin spent all day looking for worms
for its young and flew home exhausted in song.

There is Nothing, Except

When feet have acknowledged
        dust and mud as perpetual coat,
have accepted cutting through the muck field
        to reach the gravel road
to shortcut home, when hands
        have found their way out of pockets
and swung for the first time besides the hips
        and shoulders stopped hunching
from the heat the head can no longer carry,

        you will wash, you will wade
in the water freed from your clothes
        and rinse the dirt that has held you
and scrub off the mud that has bound,
        you will say goodbye to the earth
that has grown you, will know
        there is nothing except this perpetual
washing of Whitewater Creek, immersion,
        the rising wet and perfected.

Mudroom

The heavy boots, borrowed, the snow thick,
a shovel in bare hand, the Dalmatian like dominoes
on a white table, a trail of wood chips and sawdust
from the barn and Mrs. Spann sweeping,
not looking up, the dawn blue sky fabulous
and a throng of starlings full of climb and swoop
landing on sagging power lines
ignoring the hazard of shock.

Dots of blood like pebbles marked the way.
It would be a deep dig, through a foot of snow
then three feet down, ice, sod,
but the wild dog had to be buried.
I pierced, stabbed, clanged the blade
into the earth, made a pocket more than a hole.
While the Dalmatian picked frozen ice balls
from his feet, I came to warm earth.
Steam from earth's kettle gave strange comfort--
the stiff dog would thaw in the ground,
the ground would give back to flesh
a suppleness and thickness death had taken.
I placed the dog below my feet, stepped out
of the hole, then made the soil drop, snow to cover.

I took a different route back, less direct,
nodded to Mrs. Spann as I rounded the house
to the mudroom. She did not ask
and I did not tell. The dog bleeding at the door
the night before, wild, a killer,
she had opened and closed the door
without a twinge of mercy, she said.
Her son had been sent by a captain
fresh from his training barracks
into battle and died the first day.
She cried for a year, but what did it do.

There are always more boys, more weapons,
more war, more wild dogs showing up
hungry and wounded at night at your door.

Snow Fence

Spann unrolls the snow fence
and I first lift then drag it
post to post through drifts,
the posts once dressed like scarecrows
now tilted four by fours
looking like tombstones to failure.
I alternate gloves to keep my hands
from freezing, lose more wire tacks
to the snow than I get to bite into wood.
Wisps of flakes rise from the ground
whenever the wind blows
and follow currents no differently
than water in a riverbed.

All seem to end up in our faces,
and I ask if we can't turn our backs
to the wind and work from the other side,
but Spann assures me there's an aesthetic
to have the backside of the fence
to his father's farmhouse, though what
that aesthetic is he cannot say.
The lore of yore, he says, passed down generations.

By the end we know it will not matter.
Drifts pile up against the fence.
As we look back to the beginning
the snow has already started to blow across.
When the wind stops, it piles the snow
a few feet past where the fence
was designed to impede it.

We finish what we have started,
and return to the warmth of the farmhouse
and then, just then, in the first few seconds
of warmth returning, we both feel the sting

of tacks that have pierced and clawed
and dragged against and into our fingertips,
crisscrossed with jabs and penetrations,
as if a form of secret writing.

By night, the snow we meant to forbid
has found its way to the door.
In the morning our sore fingertips
rub against our thumbs as if wings
across a beak in grooming.

Vigil

I couldn't tell if he said enjoy your vigil
or your Virgil, for I had Georgics in my hand
when I came to do the watch, a weak moon
overhead, the ground freshly tilled
and grass uprooted by wild pigs
that had somehow missed the garden square.
I had no gun, but the long loping lines
of Virgil if recited loudly I knew could make
the pigs run just as many a student had.
Poems of Charles Wright peeked from inside
the book ripped from a journal
for a casual read, the same manner in which
they sounded as if they had been written,
but it was that tone that sunk deeply,
gave me measure of myself like an anchor
thrown over while fishing on a lake
and you watch the rope uncurl and run
and sizzle against the oarlock, a mist
rising from the whorls as friction and heat
raise a vapor. It was that vapor I hoped to find
that night of my watch, and when the pigs came
all grunt and swarm, rubbing against each other
in a mad meander, I could see the first boar
raise his head and sniff, the others push forward
like children who put their hands on the leader's back
afraid of what the one in front might find,
feet ready to go back, noses ready to go forward
depending on the leader's lean.

In that quiet diminutive light I could see that same vapor
rising from the boar's back, a vapor
of use, of even pleasure perhaps, muscular,
so in that one wild pig had a sense of both Wright
and Virgil, of the boar as the plow person
reaping the goodness of the earth.

I wanted to let them pass, to rip the unripe pumpkins
and gourds from their stems, to plunder
the remaining gourds and proliferate squash,
knock down the stalks of corn and trample
the furrows into an evenness in which water
would finally pool, rest and not run into the soil.

When the boar took a few steps the hair on my neck
seemed to rise and a tingle took its time
before taking over my scalp. I dropped the book
and picked up the three-pronged pitchfork.
The pigs who had watched me stretch from a seated statue
to a defensive scarecrow paid to heed,
but it was enough that I had risen, and the snorts
withdrew, the square of autumn harvest preserved.
In two nights next they would return on another's watch
and complete their task, and skunks would gather
to finish what the pigs had left.

When I returned it was nearing the fullness of darkness,
only a lash of moon left in the waning cycle.
I had expected nothing more than demolition
but again, saw steam, rising over the patch,
and however meaningless and mechanical that mist,
it gave me tie to thousands of years of plowing
both of soil and word, and I took that pitchfork
not to scare but turn the soil and rake, to scrape
the remnants not even desired by the pigs
into a pile a fire could consume in morning.
It seemed appropriate to end the watch by smoke.

Near Lime Pond

Starlings swarm over unused wires,
black pixels against the ground fog,
seeking a shake of grain
or a seed forgotten by wild turkeys.
Unharvested cranberries glow
like embers under the ice,
as if they will burn all winter,
and a single wide rake stands apparent
now that winter has revealed the thicket.

It is late afternoon, and we can feel
the darkness around the corner
as the temperature drops,
the wind whips and walls radiate
a soft copper glow that belies
their frozen state. When we enter
the house, we turn a burner on
though we have not decided what to heat,
kettle, a pan, a pot full of soup,
just to know the flame can beat back winter.
We talk about the midnight blue
of the water and the cranberries
buried under ice, like stars
we will configure into constellations
to tell a winter's story.

Signature

Venturing out at dawn, I had hoped to find
the new-fallen snow untrammeled,
but already spied a trail of small boots
between my neighbor up the hill
and a lonely maple in the swale,
two hundred steps or more.

I could tell the left foot dragged
and the right foot punched
a clean impression in the snow,
that my neighbor struggled in a drift,
and tired on the way back, the distance
shorter between the steps
until no stride at all appeared,
measured by the distance of undisturbed snow.

The day sparkled, shined, made
everything dead look new.
In the leave-less maple a hanging
seed-packed bell of suet rang with song
as chickadee, nuthatch and finch
had the fat and seeds in full swing.

In a few seconds, I knew more about my neighbor
then I had ever known,
not her name, her elder status,
jobs held, children labored,
what she couldn't cook or housekeep,
her constant critique of her spouse,
wit, a long, left arm up to wave a greeting.

I had learned of her otherness,
the part of her soul, to use a word
now damned into antiquity
that we do not share with others,

a holiness that our hearts do not tell,
a small moment of tenderness and will
by the signature of boot tracks on the snow.
She was the one who brought forth song
when the world had meant to silence it.

By Moving I Remain

Removing a Gate

Maidenhair ferns at my feet
seem to rise out of the dust for rain,
the sword ferns sprawl to catch fog,
and the maple lifts itself out of the soil,
massive roots becoming visible
like the muscles of a shirtless powerlifter.

I have taken the widowed boards
of the gate and saved them from the fire
to build a little eave that shelters
the dahlias from full sun,
and now brushed by the breeze
this creates they nod thank you
thank you thank you,
and I wonder what I can do
for travelers weary from the dust,
a small jug, a metal cup, a wooden bench.

I have wood leftover,
and the sun still to set.

Two Nights Past the Summer Solstice

I wanted daylight to stretch out
then get stuck like a clock
with damaged hands

that North America's June aura
would last into July
August September

that the fall in temperature
could occur but long summer days
would prevail into autumn

literally carry the day
despite the spin
of the globe on its axis

but then I thought
of the people south
of the equator trapped

in the time of winter darkness
week after week rising
to streetlight commuting

and I wanted them
to know that at eight o'clock
at night hummingbirds

yet hovered over agapanthus
and cats wandered
exhausted from watching wings

that the most remarkable
moths began to end slumber at nine
and looked for my exact doorway

to hover near the faux lamp
to remind me of adoration
that deer that had been hiding

in the small arbor
of my neighbor stepped out
timidly to cross

to where they'd sleep,
that children grew tired
in a natural way as the fuel of play

lowered combustion
to warm embers
that I could finally hold

that the people south
of the equator could know
how hard I loved

how hard the love
of my life loved me
in the quiet moments

when the sun set
and the cacophony
of summer with it

how I had learned
to let go the grip on light
to not seize the day

to give it away
how generosity
was meant to endure

and they would know
six months later
to give it back

Trestle

We had gone as far as the trestle that led to the pond
with its rickety boards and missing wood
        that left holes to look down into the creek
and wondered if we had enough daylight left

to walk across and watch the sunset
sparkle the water, the few geese swim
        without wake, the duckweed once brilliant
turn to a lesser shade of neon.

The dog wanted to run across, frightened
of the tremor of loose footings,
        naked bolts and crossbars,
but head up, seemingly aware of each paw-trap,

yet never slipped, not in gracefulness,
but in awkward strides, in the manner a tether
        of a boat in a storm pulls taut, relaxes,
pulls taut, and the boat lurches, survives the storm.

Emerson's divine animal came to mind,
the body, but our mind and eyes
        looking into the near future
were too far from ground to be trusted.

Perhaps the republic has traveled
just so, ignoring the missing architecture,
        the gaps in justice and equality,
a trestle made for the train of commerce

but not the evened path for others.
Perhaps we have wanted not bliss
        but ignorance, pretending not to look,
to keep our heads trained and vision up.

My mother told me often as I wiped dishes
to only see the good in people
       because the bad will be evident
whether you try to see it or not,

and perhaps that is like crossing
an old trestle, a blithe unawareness
       until your sole fails to find firmament
and your ankle scrapes against a ragged board.

The dog feels tremors, and moves.
If we avoid seeing, we plunge.
       We choose to cross. For the others
who traipse this trestle, I count the missing

and damaged planks that float without anchor,
the planks with wooden spirit worn
       and split, make a date to return,
a list of lumber and coated common nails,.

Prayer Shawl

At the crest of the mountain
a penitent in open prayer,
kneeling, weeping, raising his arms,
and not a single bird.

The winter rain has erased
all the footprints of good weather
visitors, and will mine.

Below a woman runs,
her breath visible in short puffs,
then disappears. How long
I have worn this mountain.

One Rung Down

Today, climbing to trim the plum,
I step on the highest rung
on the quivering ladder,
then withdraw, danger expressed
in the raised letters of warning—
This Is Not a Step.
But to place one foot
and then another,
to climb to the level
your shins have lost
a bar to brace against,
to face without fear—
this must be the power that preachers
and prophets feel,
that electric rush of instability
atop pyramid or mountain,
that choice between balance
below and zealous ascension.
And yet I reach.

I curl my fingers around
a greening branch and test
that highest rung,
and with my hand planted surely
around the tether of the plum,
sense that I am safe,
though I do confess to headiness,
like sitting on a three-legged stool
after a couple of drinks
when the floor swells
and breaks beneath.

Do I dare try the highest step?
The honest truth is that I tried,
I tried still connected to earth

through that darting plum branch
and felt released, and when I let go
and stood for one moment, not more,
untethered, hands out and imploring
air for balance, I was not free,
I was blinded by the fear of falling,
I was blinded by the fear of flying.

I have learned my rung of comfort
and I have learned my sense of truth,
the difference in what I can hear
and the difference in what I will speak.
I know now how far I can climb.
I could tell you what I saw that moment
I stood on the final rung untied to earth,
I could tell you grand visions
and I could tell you gripping stories
and I could tell you of tragedy
and pathos and anger and of love
overwhelming, bitterness removed,
that I joined blackbirds swarming
in joyous routes unready to land,
but the truth, the honest truth is
I saw nothing, remember only
the comfort of my left foot touching
the second rung down,
and, where it belonged,
my right foot right behind it.

Midas

A hot day, and I on hands and knees
        protecting tulips
and pansies from predators
        needing a breather,
and next to my nose
        a hippopotamus-shaped
black bee wallows
        in a red tulip, stuck
like a jumbo jet
        on the tarmac of petals,
an aerial pack mule
        with legs like saddlebags
stuffed full of sepal milt
        he cannot lift, stamen-stuck.

He required altitude,
        lift capacity,
untethering from the helipad
        of pollen-anther,
yielding his wealth for flight,
        yet an hour later
when I checked back
        he still writhed, clicking,
fumbling in his riches,
        cup-rolling in the tulip,
golden powder
        showering the air.
I would have nudged him out
        with a tender index
but found myself
        with a twinge of envy.

Let him luxuriate, for once.
        Let him forget
the zigging and zagging

and data on the garden's
grid for the hive.
Let him fill his follicles
fully, in folly.
I have, and tulips
die swiftly.

Jonah

It's a body of water without name, a short run,
not a wide creek or small river though about the size,
not a pond or a lake because the water
migrates from one elevation slowly downhill then disappears,
not caught up in a granite bowl or a limestone quarry
or swallowed by or merged in a larger flow.

Mappers for the state decided it too small to name,
the few letters on the page too long for water's length.
It starts from an artesian spring on Buller's farm
and shallows and swells as it gets to Anacker's
where one cannot leap across and in late spring
cows must wade to find their trail.

It does not empty itself into a lake like a worshipper
into a god, just runs out without settling,
or perhaps best described as runs in,
hides in the ground and never comes out,
like my childhood neighbor
thought to be mentally arrested,
a condition we now might call autistic,
who played an elusive version of kick-the-can
with my brother and me under the streetlights
near Memorial Park, sweat pasted to his shirt,
wordless, grinning. That night he disappeared
into his house and the next day
was nowhere to be found,
his father, mother, sister saying
he had to be taken away,
unable or unwilling to say who or what
had done the taking, as if some force
had swallowed him, Jonah in the whale,
but had never belched him back to life.

Some have tried to make a name for that water,
but for generations no name has taken hold,

like a baby miscarried that everyone remembers
and no one talks about, carrying a grief
which grounds him or her or them into the nameless.
All of us have parts of our lives that start
and disappear, parts we wanted to go onward,
parts we want to merge into a greater awareness,
a larger body, be a stem that fed into something greater,
a victory, a community, an art, a place in history,
to escape from one place, to disappear,
then find our mission in a larger world.

This water, nameless, I name agua de la gente,
aqua populo, dŵr y bobl, water of the people,
Jonah, I name it Jonah,
that we who are swallowed like this water,
anonymous, may emerge with a name.

Question for Van Gogh

1/

At three a.m. the sonic wash
of manufactured ocean sounds
do not impede the dendritic hallucination
of a sotto voce note of a castrato
in the halls of a dark monastery—
tinnitus, my neural artesian
of everlasting sonar,
doppelganger of sound.
I want to cauterize the axons
and eviscerate the synapses,
but what I can hear
I hear. I have come to think of it
as a homing signal, but to what flock
of emancipated pigeons escaped
from my thoughts I cannot say.

2/

A chisel Michelangelo could not imagine
enters my ear to chip the calcium nodes
hanging like stalagmites to relieve
the sea-cavern roar that 24/7 rushes,
as if I live underwater, tossed in the kelp
like an otter, stirrups and anvils perpetually
hushed in their striking, coated with cold.
I hear the chisel like a mini-jackhammer
and the surgeon is a blue-collar worker
repairing a clogged artery on the street.
In recovery, I cannot tell if I imagine
the violin but the pounding timpani
in my chest tells the truth—
still the siren wails.

3/

At twenty-six, Beethoven heard
a single violin note held
that would not diminish, decrescendo,
persevered through punishment,
wrote his third symphony though the note
had become a chord in his fourth
when it drifted from high C to middle.
It is the opening clash of the fifth
when we hear what he could not,
the low rumble that he knew by resonance
and not by pitch, and by the Hallelujah ninth,
his hearing gone, his conversations
recorded in cursive between visitors
and friends, only then did he transcribe
the holy strain through all the scales.

4/

Constant as a desert wind, the sound.
I imagine colorless tents
rolling like Pacific waves
that are anything but pacific,
Sufi mystics selling sheaves
of hilarity and laughing magi
taking shekels from ears
at the corner of the bazaar,
men devoured by unruly beards
and women only showing their eyes
whistled to by every standing pole
that withers in the wind.
Come, I call, take the shekel
from my ear, perhaps the whistle
I have will go with the coin.
Come, I call, chant a mystical poem
full of puns and humor and love
and perhaps the tone will realize
it is from God and go back to God

and leave me in peace.
For a second, it merges with the wind
and all I hear is the wind
and the flea market, yard sale, bazaar
become one with waving sine.
O God, I am free, free!
I laugh, I pull unimaginable scarves
from my sleeve, make cards
jump back into their deck,
make a camel fit through the eye of a needle.

5/

If I carve out my ear to still
the whistle of the eternal teapot,
if I have the aural nerves burned,
will I still remember
the whispering love from my wife
as we lay huddled after passion
or the soft encouragement,
the almost silent prayers?
Will I remember the claxon of the crow
or the democracy of rain,
the wild grains in the wind
like a shushing librarian?
Will I remember my daughters' breathing
as I carried them from the beach
asleep on both shoulders,
or my son's wheezing as asthma
tried to stifle his lungs,
or the quivering tremolo of my mother
as she withered toward death?

6/

When I go crazy, Vincent,
when I see the stars flame
will I still hear the colors shift?

Keel and Song

Even now, amid hatred, violence,
self-achievement and greed,

I raise my head in the morning
like a small bird below the large feeder

watches the jumble of others arrive,
snatch, and depart swiftly

before a raptor lands and sweeps a wing
to scatter fluff, flax, and millet.

Amid flutter and chirp, keel and song,
a new day's light, I am grateful.

Using Rust as Pigment

by pigment
I do not mean the purple of the wing
            or the hand-neglected plums
pierced by woodpeckers
                        and two western meadowlarks
            eviscerating the magenta skin
on a lower branch
bobbing toward dirt,
            an ochre footprint in the curving arc
of the mucky road scurrying the quail
                        across the wounded earth,
            nor the yellow of the yarrow,
nor do I mean the shadows
            of nuance, the play of light
by slats of dark among our desires,
                        I mean the bursting of pure light,
            the breaking of principle
bent by mercy,
by the grace
            of rust, the red
of rust in translucent summer,
                        iron falling apart an oxidized pigment
            the Romans used in paint,
bolts, screws,
hardware gone soft
            with the same oxygen we breathe
to live—it softens metal, hardens us.
                        A rustic shack rumples
            in decay like a deflating tent
or an overused sofa.
            Lichen grows serious, stretching
like old men's beards,
defiant,
            industrious, unkempt,
                        Ancestors appear not in dreams

but a father in the sweep of arms,
a limping gait,
        a mother in a rush of words,
                an uncle's joke that harmed,
        the musty smell
                of old books and closets
at a grandmother's house.

I had thought
thinking by now
        would be more linear, less indented,
perhaps shiny with wisdom, coined,
                not the burnished penny
        in the silent fingertips of exchange.
When I write
silence
        I do not mean the peace after the crow's caw,
the catcalls of the raven
                from unused telephone poles.
        They make sound but do not disturb
what is silent,
what moves deeply
        without pounding the timpani of the ear.
When I say
silence
                I mean the inaudible tow
        of our ancestors in the stream
of summer, how they rise
        in thought but never surface
like logs
too heavy to float
                and too light to sink,
        pressuring underneath our thoughts
and emotions but incapable of bursting in on them.

        By rust I mean on this longest day
how quiet

this lasting light
                depends on the lost,
      their slow oxidation,
the longing
to enter the trees
      and to hear, to finally hear
the history of grief, of light
                expanded into the color of love,
      to see how we live awake
like a hummingbird sleeps
      wings finally folded,
throat raised skyward
                gulping for air.

By Moving I Remain

My thighs make a swath
through the switches and bramble,
tugged, yanked, stuck,
as if this gnarled angry chaos
wanted to snare, entrap,
twirl and catch like barbed wire
curled around a heifer that dared
to batter the fence and zing
the staples shot out and the wire
recoiled and you find the hide
and stagnant hoof of the cow.

But I am too old to be stagnant.
I press forward to the yawning light
ahead, the red truck on the dirt road
waiting like a falling sun,
allowing the thorns their cotton twills,
the snags, pricked flesh,
worn patches a marker of pleasure.
By moving I remain.

Holsteins at Equinox

I walk with Holsteins ambling
barn-ward down a dark March trail,
their stretched and sagging udders
swaying like sloops in the harbor
at high tide, trudging the trail
with psychological interpretations
shining off their black
and white splotches of hide,
eyes bulging like full moons
newly risen from the wage
of war on gravity, their paycheck
an empty udder from seventy
pounds they sacked around.
We cross the meridian of muddy spring
into the dried dust of summer.

At the barn I will warm the jets that suck
the milk so they don't get shocked
and kick, and know which side
a cow prefers, how long
the tepid wash should take,
the number of free squirts
I can give the cats
with the last unhitched nipple.
The cows will grow content
with the stroke of wooing speech,
of song, and truth be told
I like the tone of my own voice
when talking to a Holstein,
and remind myself, when coach,
to coo in soft chromatic scales.
For now, the bell cow leads,
and I follow her home.

Passage

Near wavering asphalt
I let the pendular scythe coast to a stop:

two boys are picking prodigious berries,
thorns pricking their almond arms;

honey colors the white wall
of an empty two-story lodge—

the pleasure of merely seeing,
that subliminal and delicate tie

of inner self and other,
the wide sweep making voyeur participant,

the sense in my cells
of the pulsing hive of wings,

the taut plump flesh of berries
bursting tart and sweet in my mouth,

memory of golden arms
stung by blackberry branches

as I swept the thorns from my face
mingling my blood with the blood of berries—

and my wife comes to greet me
shaking heat from underneath her cotton dress

aware I have this preference for motion
which arrests.

The Root Endures

The Infinitive to Listen

Threatened by the sprawl of an oak
and unremitting sun
the timber and truss of the roof age,
crack, dry and rot,
the roofline no longer an erect V,
sides sagging as if the ink
that drew them had become wet
from the winter's rain.

I spy bumps and swales in the linear run—
squirrels have planted acorns
in the shingles, pushing up a corner
of a square and tamping down,
but the shingles appear more like
Fedoras with the brim curled from overuse
of a gripping tip of acknowledgment.

I have lived here too long, perhaps,
to go on explaining to prospective buyers
about picking holly sprigs
bent over the eaves in the winter
and how one has to dress the outside lights
from the power feed and grounding hub
on the roof or risk a sudden electrical flip,
flop and pitch to the yard below,
the dent in the gutter from a branch
of the cedar across the street that sailed
like a straw in the gusts of a winter storm,
the little pocket in the beam
where a chickadee had her nest
and a crow or jay could not pierce,
the flat area where in spring
one year recovering from a torn calf
I bathed in sunlight and read Chinese poetry
until I saw every bush, shrub

and stripling as an ideogram,
learned how complicated
the pen-stroke graphic
of the infinitive to listen is,
with speaker, hearer, past
and present, whispers
and blares of vocables
held in a single image,
with not a single vowel,
phoneme or syllable
to explain the entirety of to listen.

We have no heirs to this house,
only to our home, which travels
in the lives of our children.
I have learned this roof is a brushstroke
that cannot be spoken.

The Large Swales in the Road

You jerked your head around
when you read the sign
Depression Ahead, drove
forward, and now you were.
You noticed them everywhere,
the large swales in the road
that when young and your father
drove at a speed your mother disliked,
they gave you a lift from gravity
and a thrilling scrape of the undercarriage,
sparks flew one time your neighbor said.
Your parents could not afford
the speed of a flickering movie,
so flew lightly over the earth.

Today that's why you went out driving,
looking for that little lift from gravity,
that startling loss of your stomach
as speed and fulcrum launch you
from the pull of the earth, to joy.
Hadn't your father always been sad
that he could not continue the cheating
of downward attraction?
Your mother held back her delight,
a soft smile cracking her lips
as she turned her face to the window
so that you and your siblings could not see?
Even in deficiency using this bump-shot
to elation was like a carnival ride
your family could never afford,
a short weak thrust against time,
the body lost in elation,
mind suspended, the soul
in the swirl of timeless wonder.

So you speed up, look for a large swale
to rise for an instant, your legs
avoiding the drag of gravity,
your brain floating
in the skull for a moment
mindless, and thankful,
of your continued poverty.

The Other Shoe

Like some careless mammoths
I step into the melting lake of tar
on the street, but lucky my life—
I lose a shoe, yet do not sink into eternity.
What do the shadowed drivers think
when they pass that sunlit shoe,
swerve to avoid, run right over?
Why just one shoe? Isn't that the question?

When we see two shoes connected
by their laces thrown over a power line
above the street we comprehend
the toss and glee that put them there.
but a single shoe that caught the wire
and held? How long did it take to do?
Or perhaps the mystery is what took
the other shoe, the asphalt

without the pairing match.
It bothers, as if the one has been abducted,
or perhaps discarded
in a ditch, and we think of kids' faces
on milk cartons, and imagine a post
of a shoe, just to mate one back with another.
My father said after my mother died
that he felt he had lost a leg,

that he limped, could not find good footing
on the pavement, that a wire
had been strung between his limbs
for life and without her on the other end
he seemed unconnected, off balance,
able to trip and fall. Though he lived
another eleven years he never found
the other shoe.

I stand on the curb and see my shoe
stuck in the tar like a memorial.
I could return and wrench it back,
but I know why tar exists,
why mammoths died, but to stoke
the fire of curiosity, of remembrance,
of sympathy for those shoes without their other,
I let it stick.

One-way, Out and Only

I watch the hikers come and go but never their return—
    we live on a one-way, out and only,
wending to campsites a mile away,
    called a loop but not in the manner of a circle
but a helical coil with start and termination.
    They ask how far it is, and knowing they are stuck
until it ends I tell them not much farther,
    a few bends, a climb, and then in the way a messiah holds
his followers, promise the everlasting downhill walk.

One day, I dream, someone will turn an ankle
    and re-turn our way, or a nest of wasps will burst
from a well-placed stick from an errant hand
    and all those hikers from all those years
will come running back in front of me
    like water forced uphill must settle finally at my feet.

I think of all the braided girls and ponytailed women who vanished,
    the dads in new tennis shoes ill fit for woodruff trails,
the cocky boys all bluff and swagger
    who'd be drained of piss and vinegar
by the sight of a bobcat tail.
    Instead, I collect the chapstick tubes and trail mix bags
the crows and stellar jays inspect.

I'd like to plant a sign that says
    "REMEMBER TO COME BACK THE WAY YOU CAME"
and I suppose that's the way I want all things to go,
    steel returned to iron ore on Lake Superior ships,
paper back to pulp, pulp to wood,
    wood to tree, Gulf Stream to Mississippi River
to Fox River to Crawdad Creek to the little spring

near Highway 23 where I kneeled and drank water
    just above the temperature of ice,

my mother now dead from cancer kneading an apron like bread
     anxious that the world would snatch
me up, and lure me away.
     I would like to tell her that it has.

Four Novembers

Child

My parents could not promise when we arrived
that we would not stay put for good

for they were experts at leaving, a hug,
a wave, an overloaded car

following the moving van as if we did not know
where it was headed

but wherever it was headed was good enough.
Our crying stopped in the distance

between our town and the next.
My mother said the friends we lost we would gain back

except they'd be new faces in new places.
But as we moved to the next place

the number diminished, until at the end of the moves
there were no friends left.

My father said we always had each other, but then
I left in November.

Spouse

I chose to fast on Thanksgiving, took a narrow road
east from the college to an esker

where Ojibwe drummed and I drank so much tea
I jittered, clenched my teeth and muscles

and beat my feet to an awkward rhythm. I could not dance.
I had lived ten lives in ten towns until college

and the constant docking, mooring, unmooring at one town
for the next made me travel lightly

as if I had stored my heavy possessions at my parents' home
and would return for them later. I never returned.

When I married, I carried my bride into an apartment
and felt in my arms the weight of my life,

a joy I could forever suspend, inhabit,
a transiting home that stayed in one place.

Grandmother

My grandmother died before Thanksgiving
so the memorial had turkey, potatoes, and squash.

It snowed so heavily only a few men and myself in a truck
went to the cemetery to bury the casket.

She had spoken in tremolo, a fluctuating and warm sound,
and in the blizzard the memory of her voice

seemed to clear the road. The next day under more snow
the road could not hear her voice any longer.

Since that November, I have been searching for the road
that carried her song, which burned off the cold,

through one town and the next, never settled,
a Main Street, a side street, a lane the wind could empty.

Father

After my mother died, I walked a path in a field of reeds
with my father to an opening in a marsh

where geese and egrets congregate before flying south.
Wisdom had once flown out of his mouth,

but wit and humor had left him, and the following spring
when I returned, the geese had not come back, and never would.

Barn, Moth

The roll of the earth extinguishes
      the last flame of daylight,
            a pitch, a yaw, then night.
A moth tumbles through
      the incandescent light
            of the yard lamp
into that indeterminate
      strip of obscurity
            where radiance diffuses
into absence and reflection,
      thin smooth glass
            that shines like a jar
holding the glow of harvest
      and beyond the unlit cornfield
            and darkness of my longing.
I miss your voice,
      at times a bellicose bar
            beating against the metal of time
at times a filament drawn so thin
      one electric word wired to another
            brings radiance to all around it.

At the Window in Spring

The cool air slips under the door,
sheetrock chill to the touch,
insulation fallen between walls
like saggy trousers without a belt.

When I sit by the window in the dark
I pin my cheek against the cold pane,
returning to watch the blossoms of the plum
flutter like moths in the moonlight,
and for a moment I am airborne as well.

I have been carried by many for so many years.

Everything Rural Will Be Razed

Past the patina
of buckboards
grayed, grains
weeping black
resin, porous

crooked rafters
broken barn
truss and beam
perch for mock
and crow curse

jagged glass
bending light
yet color absent—
put the camera
away, for the lens

cannot capture
the source
of land's weeping—
everything rural
will be razed

sometimes
out of brokenness
beauty
but now
only brokenness

Richland Centre, Wisconsin

A hard person with people
can be softened
by a swale of grass,
an undulant hill.

We Will Never Mend This

The last heron died in the weeds
of the San Lorenzo River
in a spoon-shaped backwater,
its beak that struck the skein of the pool
and pierced the gleaming images below
now a short spear on a frame without feather or flesh,
neck concealed by fallen reeds
as if the green world's attempt at a blanket of concealment—
that death did not sadden,

that the skeleton of a frog lodged at the top
of the heron's torso, legs curled back and stuck
as if trying to hide from the act of engorgement,
the way a kidnapped child pretends in fetal tuck
that violence cannot find him,
the way a woman curls to fend the blows
her drunken man provides,
that death did not sadden,

that I also had this knot wedged below my throat
obstructing my breath, jammed, lodged
and not slipping down or wasting away,
a rock of sorrow wedged into a space
constricting my lungs from gathering a clean breath,
like an oversized frog trapped among feathers,
that all of this was no coincidence,
this recognition, this hole by bare hands
dug in the mud on the side of the river
and the bones and the beak sliding softly,
feathers separating, frog displaced
into a separate depression, that internal death
did not sadden, but the knot
coming apart, the grief following,
hands rinsed in the river, the bizarre
and beautiful bounty of life diminishing,
everything at once coming unstitched--

We will never mend this.

Written On Walt Whitman's Birthday

> Down on the ancient wharf, the sand, I sit,
> with a new-comer chatting
> —From *Twenty Years*, by Walt Whitman

I finish the long walk to the Santa Cruz wharf
where grace pervades on a bench
when the sun burns off the fog
with Whitman chatting in my ears,
hear his tones on the wood and steel
in thrums of arrhythmic leather,
soles of rubber squeaking like clarinets,
and I think he'd like the collar-less throng
in tennis shoes and cheap sandals,
uncoordinated jazzy high-pitch roast of leisure
among the regular grind of work,
how he'd listen to my life and pull me from the wind
like an anonymous tuft and weave me into the fabric
of a nation, turn anomie into bonhomie,
how, with head bent down from the enormous weight
of inclusive thought, he'd exalt the beautiful
ugliness of toes, long for warm bowls of water,
soapsuds, and a thousand hands rubbing feet.

To My Child

The white-and-black lilies are too heavy to loft in the wind.
Water's expensive and rare, but we have shared
it with the lilies so they do not become shriveled bloom,
waxed petals pollen-strewn arid and wilting.
It is we who look diminished, our showers spaced
and short, our dishes stacked in the sink
waiting for the right day to wash.
I lose track of how long it has been
since I didn't pray for rain.

When I taught you about stars,
I said there were millions, gazillions,
that someday we could reach a count,
but what I meant was to look up in awe, amazement,
yet here I am stuck in the dark looking at the large dipper
and counting, and counting on, only three stars
in a handle and four to make a rectangular cup.
I am praying for rain in a sideways manner,
the way a coyote sidles up a street
hoping I can reach the handle and tip it
forward, make that ill-formed cup
you'd think pounded out in metal
pour whatever it contained.

I want to tell you of this stupidity of mine
so you will be prepared for the night
when you are deprived by death, loss,
separation, cancer, even love,
and look skyward into the starry sky
and forget awe, and focus on a single light,
and wish, and wish, and wish.
It will be okay to do that, to pray,
to extend the desperation of your thoughts
into space and attempt to configure
a constellation into satisfying our desire
knowing that it will not.

It is, after all, the better part of being human,
why we look up and out
at least half of the time, to search
what cannot give to give to us,
why I sat with my mother breathless
from cancer asking her a story to tell
of her youth that she could not remember,
or asked a homeless man
how his day was going.

I know, as you will, that you cannot tip
the handle, the cup will not pour,
but you need to know you will try,
and you will keep on trying,
and learn it is not the failure of praying
but the triumph of continuing to ask.

Walking Zayante Sandhills

It is surprising how good
the stony soil feels on your feet
and the respite the clay, cold
and always wet, gives your soles,
the thin paddles of your toes.
Pebbles slip as your feet
step down, form a surface
more fluid than solid stuff
should be, and I think this is
not the mountain the great ones
have trod, Jesus, Moses,
Muhammad, Zarathustra,
this is not dry and ascetic,
and it is surprising how good
it is to feel, to take in
all the smooth feathered wings
of woodcocks beating water
and coots winnowing pondweed,
the pistil-coupled
bee-dappled plums,
the shale-streaked soil
beaded with a day's sweat
and the sinew of blackberry
vine and ivy, the ivory
cast of cartilage and bone
in the early evening light,
and it should feel like this
for everyone, the rock-rimmed
and roiling sky studded
with fluffy tussocks
snorted and puffed
out of the western rookery,
a plunging bloody red
dropping to cold rock,
and out of the white bones

of oak broken
by hatchet-head and heft
a woodpecker bursting
through spines of sunshine
and ribs of shadow,
loganberry poking
through thorn-choked wires
of a trampled fence like notes
in the margin of a book more fruitful
than the limbs of lines, branches
of text, the furling, unfurling
flight of the woodpecker echoed
by the two-beat booming in my chest.

The Root Endures, a Poem From Home

We were collegiate court jesters
juggling the putrid fruits
      of a kingdom gone to greed,
not the priests of a purifying politic
free of polemic. I have no remorse.

Amid our middle-class neighbors
housed in coffins of quiet
      and lull stilled by specters
of money and phantoms of power,
we were wolves in the rough,

we spoke from the throat
and thought the mind and viscera
      were housed lower than the tongue
and higher than the heart.
We howled.

We thought nothing could keep us silent.
Our lips were warlords
      of promise, we were wanderlusts,
gusty and new, we were the myth,
our lives were belief,

speaking and speaking loudly
the only truths.
      But in years the trumpet
of my voice died, the throat
became parched ground

when the lake of my heart went dry.
It was so easy to think that we owned
      not one square inch of the earth
and yet the hard daily drag of my feet
told me I had been allotted

a small plot and my lungs
owned a portion of air
     in which to find a peaceful place
to work out my life,
to live out my work.

I was not brave enough
to be a major martyr,
     or not brave for a long enough time,
and the severity of my character
served only in a negative way,

in insolent but quiet abnegation,
in what I could refuse to do.
     My integrity stood rich, my fortitude poor.
Though the radical in me still longs
for the killing prison,

the guerrilla in me has long since waned.
In another country perhaps.
     Unable to change the fabric of the nation
I have been able to save wetlands and marsh,
planted three thousand pine and cedar,

and taught a willing few how to read.
I have not moved any mountains
     or been more than a daisy in a chain
of flowers against the nuclear powers,
easily unlinked,

nor been diligent at lowering wealth
to higher worth.
     It is true the frontiers the heart
and mind had established
the mouths and hands and feet

will never reach, the rivers
they will never ford,
        and it is true no grand symphonies
proceed from my lips,
for my songs are only poems

short and occasional.
But late at night on the rug
        with my wife and children,
the spare words and humble rhymes
have a majesty and meaning

we never could have known,
and in these words I conserve the land,
        the inheritance of democracy
free from probate and tax,
lives led by the pristine chorus

of concern and not the polluted cant
of chemical, cosmetic, and coin.
        The grand themes and high theory
have a smaller and later development,
for what I longed for at twenty-four

has begun to happen,
not the fusion nor revolution
        we sought ardently for, but an enhancement,
perhaps, of those themes, which,
once taken root, like ivy, persist.

About the Author

Jeff Burt grew up in rural and small-town Wisconsin, with a boyhood dominated by fields and water, Lake Superior, Lake Mason, the Fox River and its tributaries, Long Lake, and the Mississippi. He has lived in Northern California for most of his adult life, sculpted by redwood and hardwood forests, fires, droughts, earthquakes, and the Monterey Bay. He and his wife live in Santa Cruz County, where his three children grew and were released into the wilds of other places.